QUOTE ME

ESHAM ABDUL GILES

QUOTE ME

WRIITTEN BY ESHAM ABDUL GILES

EDITED BY TAWANDA THOMAS

Cover Design by BAJA UKWELI

For further information about this book, write all inquires and permissions to;

Focus Write Inspire LLC.

PO BOX 373

NEWARK, NJ 07101

www.FocusWriteInspire.com

Library of Congress Cataloging-in-Publication Data is available.

Library of Congress Control Number: 2013936781

ISBN-13: 978-0-615-79537-9

Also by
ESHAM ABDUL GILES

PROLIFIC POETRY

eAG

esham abdul giles

Quote Me

DEDICATION

TO EVERYONE!

PEACE, LOVE AND BLESSINGS

QUOTE ME

I quote how I live it,

I quote how I see it,

I quote how things deeply affect me as a human being.

What makes sense to me may or may not make sense to you,

Or maybe a quote here or there can associate with something you've been through.

I quote how I live it,

I quote how I see it,

I quote how things deeply affect us as human beings.

Right or wrong; Truth or rare,

I know there is some out there.

Who can quote from here to compare?

How they live, or how they see,

We all use these words at some point in our life,

"QUOTE ME!"

QUOTE ME

ESHAM ABDUL GILES

Always root for the underdog

Being viewed at a disadvantage and rising to any occasion to win is the ultimate. Never give up, even if you are labeled not to beat the odds. Hold on tight to your faith and belief in self. You will win.

So they feel I've collapsed? No! I've grown up.

Can something positive emerge from so many setbacks? Positive things don't always emerge from collapse but they can. Things can grow into healthy landscapes minus pollution. It's a new beginning for starting over. Do not allow petty jealousies to pollute.

—

If my mission is Pluto and yours is the Moon, you should talk with Neil Armstrong. He could further assist… As I am going further than you could ever imagine.

Never limit yourself or your expectations…If you truly believe in something, move heaven and earth to get it done.

I lived long enough to know that just living isn't good enough. You must make a statement. You must leave your mark.

Every person on this planet has an implicit reason for being here. Ask yourself, "What is my purpose? Why am I here? What am I here to do?" It surely isn't to just live. Use your gifts GOD has blessed you with to leave your impact or footprint on the world.

Don't wait for anybody to give you anything. Go out and get it yourself.

What are you waiting for? Prosperity isn't going to just fall in your lap. Get up! Reach high! You can do what you put your mind to and have whatever you want in this world.

If they can't stand to see you shine…Tell them to, look away or buy a pair of shades…because it's bright over here.

They hate you for trying. They hate you for being a go-getter. They hate you for living a life filled with happiness. They hate you for having a natural glow, an illuminating aura. Well hey; you know what you can tell them? "Get over it!" Your hate won't stop my shine.

Know your circle.

Loyalty should always be tested...Acknowledge suspicions that reveal secrets...Intentions and true colors will be revealed in time. Lock and seal this to memory.

Learn from what has failed you.

Poor choices, faulty decisions, and bad judgments can cost you. I mean that literally. Mistakes are made. Oh how I hate mistakes. I feel like I'm thinking about them forever. But if it wasn't for me making mistakes I would never have learned anything new. A life without mistakes (if this were to be possible) would most likely be stagnant, boring, and unproductive.

There's always a reason for meeting someone...good or bad, it should add value and/or perspective.

I absolutely believe that a lot of the people in our lives are there for a reason. Not everyone, but I think the people we are closest to are those that we have shared multiple decades with, and we continue working out whatever spiritual lessons we need to learn with and from them, until we finally get it sorted out. I have had many instances in my life where I have met someone and either felt instantly at ease with them, or have instantly felt that this person isn't for me...without knowing why, I knew nothing about them...at least not that I remember! But everybody you meet in life you're not going to click with. That's just the way it is. Everyone is in my life for a reason. I have learned very valuable lessons from all of them. All are good lessons but some of them hurt learning them.

Never let go of your principles.

If I compromise my principles, I would feel like a fool and wind up regretting it. Not so much based on the person or situation but because it is what it is and it's totally up to me to accept it. If I accept it, I would most likely find every fault in the person or situation. The reason being is I went against my principles. When you, too easily abandon your own principles, you lack integrity. When you refuse to compromise on the way you practice your principles, you also lack flexibility. That's something I don't know if I'm equipped to do. Your principles are the morals and values that guide and govern your life. Your principles are not so much about what you do, or how you do things, but more so, about what you believe is right or wrong. They are your personal "nonnegotiable" never bending ways for which you cannot sit down, shut up, or back off. For them your principles that is, you must take courage and stand your ground. PERIOD.

If you want or expect major success in life, you can't be afraid to take risk.

Risk taking isn't easy. It maybe uncomfortable and frightening for some. However it is the only way we can push ourselves to see how far we can go. It is the only way we learn what goals we can achieve. It is the only way we can live to our full potential and realize our dreams. Risk taking is the difference between looking back and reflecting on what we've accomplished and looking back with regret at what we wished we would have done. Win or lose, achieve or fail, I will never limit myself. I will risk it all if necessary. Those who fear risk and hold back will accomplish little or nothing at all. Those who see risk as an opportunity for potential growth, will move ahead and accomplish great things.

The best way to predict your future is to invent it. Abraham Lincoln

Some of us are just born entrepreneurs. I was never happy in my "Positions", even though I was good at what I did. When I managed someone else's business, I constantly remembered how it wasn't mine. It gave me headaches, because I knew I was making someone else rich and benefit from my time and effort. I value my time and effort and can put it into my own company. Don't sit on your hands. Get up! Create that future you want...Invest in yourself.
Entrepreneurs know that they can create their future. They just have to hold onto that belief when times are tough. They just have to get back up each time they're knocked down.

If you feel you don't deserve what you get, you may need to change things, even if it's going to be the hardest thing you'll ever do.

In order to change our direction and course in life, we have to believe that a better life, one that we know would be better for us and everyone around us is possible we have to believe we deserve it. No one can change our lives except us. If we really don't believe we're deserving of a better life, it will never become reality. Don't settle for less.

21

I'm not everyone's cup of tea...but hey, what does that matter. I'm hot and my own flavor

Not relying on the validation of others for your self-worth is a good thing. So by all means try to find the spot where you can be that kind of person. This attitude of not giving a damn what anyone thinks of you does not "elevate" you above others. You can't then turn around and say "I am better than everyone else." No, when you do this, you realize that you're no better than the idiots who are judging you. The ego in every person can judge, interpret, criticize, condemn, and analyze other people and their actions. The ego will compare it with who they are. When you realize we come from the same place and are cut from the same cloth, you know that everyone is connected. Caring what others think of you is a negative filter. Once you are free of this, you are free to care about what is important. YOU!

Thirsty is just another way of saying, "Attention seeking, Pathetic fools."

Attention-seeking behavior is surprisingly common. Being the centre of attention alleviates feelings of insecurity and inadequacy. On the contrary the relief is temporary for these thirsty jokers as their underlying problem remains unaddressed low self-confidence low self-esteem, low levels of self-worth, and a lack of self-love. I honestly believe that adults who fit the 'attention seeking' mold have always been that way, even as a child. As a child, they have either sought attention or were given attention all the time, in which as an adult they don't know how to act any other way. The child who seeks attention possibly feels neglected because of other siblings, or have parents that really don't know how to connect emotion. The child then engages in behavior that they know will get their parent's attention, be it good or bad. The other type of child is always given attention and made to feel special. This child does not know what it is like to not have attention all the time, when the child gets older and people are not paying them as much attention, they will likely react in ways to draw attention. Hence the word; THIRSTY!

Who can stop a person who never gives up?
NO ONE!

No one can cheat you out of anything in life but
yourself. Believe in yourself and your abilities. No
one can tell you what you can or cannot become.
Look completely pass, over, and around the
naysayers.

Be Careful of what you become accustomed too.

As I write my story, I realize now just how lost I was compared to how far I've come. My life is deep, my walk was deep and I see how easily one can fall into any form of addiction. It's all around us. Stay strong people.

Ego and greed will make you lose your way;
lose your common sense and cloud your
judgment.

Take what's wrong and make it right. Humble
yourself or be humbled.

Some regard discipline as a chore. For me, it's order.

Imagine what you could accomplish if you could simply get yourself to follow through on your best intentions no matter what. Picture yourself saying, "I'm going to write this book, approximately 20,000 words or 200 pages." Without self-discipline that intention won't become manifested. But with sufficient self-discipline, it's a done deal. The pinnacle of self-discipline is when you reach the point that when you make a conscious decision; it's virtually guaranteed you'll follow through on it. Take a look at the person who works two jobs owns a company and writes books. How can they do all of this you ask? They are focused and disciplined accompanied with strength, determination, and order.

I've fought many rivals...the worse were those who called themselves my friend.

If you're fighting constant battles with your friends those are not friends at all. They are fakes and pretend- to- bees. One thing I noticed with fake friends is that they hate to see you happy. If you tell them 10 positive things that you have accomplished, they will focus on the one thing you didn't. We all know misery loves company and these miserable people don't want to hear about anything but bad things that you've encountered. Then in turn they will use those very things against you. Truly sad! I once had a slew of fake friends... They don't exist anymore. They have been subtracted from my life. And you know what... I don't miss them at all. My life is infinitely better and the people I invest my time with now are the ones who make me a better person.

Pride is fueled by insecurity…dying to show others how great you are only shows how far from being great you really are.

Insecure people often reveal their self-doubt by being over- the- top and extra to a point where it's unbearable to tolerate…. The best thing to remember is that pride is fueled by insecurity I'll say a few things about what causes that condition. Many things can contribute. Critical or neglectful parents, poor academic skills, frequent moves that make you "the outcast" (especially if you are introverted by nature), learning disabilities such as ADHD, being "different" in some fashion (size, shape, color, religion), feeling ashamed of your parents or your residence, frequent rejections, getting fired or laid off (whether deserved or not), clumsiness, a history of abuse or bullying; physical unattractiveness, deformity, or injury and the like.

We have the ability and the responsibility to choose whether our actions follow a great or destructive path.

My path to greatness is responsibility. It's very easy to get on course to the wrong path; it's hard to stay on a true and righteous course. You must first know who you are. You must begin to love yourself and know your worth. You must begin to have self discipline, believe in your own values, be yourself and love yourself for everything that you are. I love myself and I believe in my abilities. That's how I stay true. Believe in what you believe in. And don't worry about others, for they will be the very ones trying to lead you into destruction.

When you're comfortable in your own skin your naturally beautiful.

If you don't feel comfortable in your own skin, who do you feel comfortable pretending to be? As you ask yourself this question you may need to take some time to find your authenticity. Beauty is never dependent upon the approval of others. Beauty is very much self-defined and self-created. The only person who can ever truthfully tell you "you are beautiful" is also the only person who can "make you beautiful." That's you!

Wrong associates will take more than they give…and leave you when they have nothing to gain or benefit from you.

Associate with people who are going to help you grow. We need to feed each other not evaporate one another. I don't care who it is; family, friend, husband, or wife. How else are we going to grow?

Stay true to yourself and all accolades and prosperity will come naturally.

You stay true to yourself by doing things for you. Never mind what other people think you should. You should know what makes you happy and content? If you don't ask yourself...then do them. That's how you stay true to yourself. I know that when I do things that are fulfilling and satisfying to myself and to others I am authentically being true to self (for example) writing this inspirational book. Don't lie to yourself no faking it, as you go along, because being fake everyday takes too much energy. However true to self is effortless

Don't sit and waste your time being stuck.

The beauty of the word passion is that for some of us we may know our passion but our timing is always wrong. Or for others, our timing is precise only to reveal that we have not found purpose in our objective. This is the process of elimination. When you find your passion and it aligns with time, you will be filled with new visions that make sense. Until then - remember sometimes to find the answer you may have to figure out the incorrect alternatives first.

Ask yourself, "Do I want to leave a mark on this world or an image?"

Great people, whether they lead small or large groups, leave a legacy that transcends them, that cements their contribution to the growth and transformation of those they inspire. My path was made to lead and give hope and voice to those who are left in the dark. I will be remembered for my work and those I've helped to inspire.

Be who you want to be! Not what the opinionated public think you should be.

Don't become something just because someone else wants you to. It won't make you happy if you do so.

Make your dreams your reality.

For much of my life I've felt like I was on the outside looking in...A young man without a clue. One who could never muster up the skill and courage to make his dreams a reality. But I sat, I wrote, I dreamed and now a sophomore book later here I am. You too can make your dreams reality...Never doubt yourself.

If you're trying to make positive changes you must keep your perspective broad, focused, goal orientated, and always positive.

Terminate the self-limiting 'I can't' and change it to 'I can & I will.'

Let nothing or no one define who you are…remember, "reputation is for those who care what people think."

Do not become defined by what others think of you; or bothered by judgment. While they sit and judge you're every move. You do what's best for you! Move to the beat of your own drum. You owe nothing to anyone; not your family, friends, or co-workers.

People spend a life time living in fear of chasing a dream or following their heart to step out on faith. I'd rather risk all to accomplish my destiny than to live a life I settled for.

Ditch the self-limiting statements. Jump in and stop playing outsider. Do something today to give discomfort a reason not to exist. Nothing can burn out my flame...I will fly with a broken wing if I have too.

My people, "Be done with **Useless Alliances.**"

We all know someone who has no goals at all. Ok sure they may have a job but everything goes out as soon as they get it. It's spent on clothes, parties and paying for the chase. This is an over broke mentality. Stay clear of this if you plan to succeed as they will take all your time and energy and try to encourage you to settle.

How can you respect someone who doesn't respect them self?

The answer is, "you can't!" The only thing I can say to those who lack self respect is, you need to know your strengths, weaknesses, and your emotions really well. You need to get more familiar with yourself and not become something that others want you to be; because that doesn't in any way show that you respect yourself. Ironically it shows you'd be willing to change just to please those around you.

Karma goes full circle…so be careful what you put out; it definitely will come rolling back around to you.

Everything we say and do determines what's going to happen to us in the future. Whether we act honestly, dishonestly, help or hurt others, it all gets recorded and it all comes back either in this life or the next.

Prayer is the cure for a lost soul,
confused mind and broken heart.

When I feel lost I turn to Him. When I feel
confused I turn to Him. When my heart was
broken I turned to Him. In good and bad times
I turn to Him. I am and forever will be a
praying man.

Life is too short not to have what you want at least once in your life.

If you're like me you sacrifice most to do what you must to make sure all your obligations are met. I'm happy doing so but I also want to do something just for me at least once.

Any form of growth begins with sight.

To grow you must broaden your horizons...go beyond what you're use too. Look at a challenge as an opportunity, a chance to grow.

Visualize your intentions.

As much as I dislike being unhappy, I've learned that discomfort can be a powerful motivator. Similarly, being too comfortable can lull me into complacency and stagnation and I definitely don't need that. I had to learn what it would take to get out of the rut...I had to visualize my intentions.

Put your mind in your heart.

Where matters of the heart are concerned things can get very, very deep. However, when it comes to loving your own heart, it's best to drop the drama (I know, easier said than done). Conflicting at times I know, it's hard to make up your mind and follow the path of your heart, but you must or you will forever be stuck.

Make your moves cautiously.

Word to the wise, always move with caution for it is easy to make the same mistake twice when moving fast. But if you learn and move accordingly, mistakes will open doors to possibilities you would otherwise have never knew existed.

I don't bow my head to later betray… I've learned my lesson from hurting people for selfish reasons.

But guess what? This mindset is pretty damn common. It just took me a while to realize this. People do it all the time. If they want something or someone no matter whose involved they are going to have it. Married? So what! You dated my friend? So what! People want what they want. This selfishness will repeat, if one doesn't grab hold of his or her self respect and soul.

Sometimes things are so cloudy that I can't see anything but grey.

In my experiences over the past couple years, I've come to realize that nearly everyone has some kind of hang up or struggle that they have severe difficulty in getting over. These struggles keep us from a fully-developed relationship with our God. We'll never be totally free from sin as long as we're here on earth, but we can be free from some of the stumbling blocks that bring us pain and suffering day after day.

What has society come to when ebonics is considered a part of normal conversation?

Who does dat? Who does what? Where dey do dat at? What! You're kidding me, right? Where do they do what? I don't know...Why you don't tell me. You can start by using proper pronunciation and dialogue. Pick up a book, not slang from a rap video.

You are not a carpet...let no one walk all over you.

Why the need to address this some may be wondering...its common sense. But not for most who confuse any form of abuse as love. I can say a lot but I will just say a few things. Do not let others discriminate you. Do not let others put you down for anything. Sticking up for your rights and yourself is very important or this world will take advantage of you and everything you got. Always open up your eyes. Always try to analyze people, and do not trust easily. Not everyone will be your friend, and not everyone will understand your point of views and what you stand for in your life. Just be who you are, stand up for yourself, and never let anybody walk all over you. Just live life, smile, and do what is right for you.

Hypocrites double talk and smile. Now can you trust someone who never keeps their mouth shut or claim they do no wrong?

While they sit there and make accusation after absurd accusation, while spewing all that blatant hypocrisy and double talk, time after time as they refuse to acknowledge any wrong doing on their part. Unfortunately these types of people never look in the mirror. They always seem to find fault or find things they won't do in everyone else but all along live a life of sin and debauchery on the grandest scale. They are the biggest fraudsters. These are sickening set of people that you don't want to associate yourself with.

If something no longer serves purpose why hang on? You will only grow frustrated with linger.

When a friendship or relationship no longer serves purpose and becomes nothing but negative and destructive you have to let it go. It's not good for your mental, emotional or physical health to stay in it. You will constantly be reminded why you should let it go. Don't put yourself through the torment because your intentions are pure and genuine while on the other side of this they're not. You have to love and respect yourself over anything other.

Bad relationships are unfortunately common.

Even worse, bad relationships are like cancer. Once you are infected, it spreads overtime to other areas of your life...I spent years trying to clean all the areas of my life that got infected. It's not easy. Believe me. But we must find strength to move on in life. Being hurt by so called friends, significant others or even family members can leave you cold and bitter.

The mind is a powerful and mysterious thing.

Everything that has happened or is happening in your life affects your mindset. Although some may see this to be a paradox of choice...my belief is that you need to refocus your energy on aspects of your life that will move you in the direction that greatly benefits you mentally and spiritually. We all can evolve into someone great. Remember, your changing ᶠᵒ the better. You're not someone immature, ⁱsguided or misinformed as to what he or she ᵼts. Grab your life my people cause, I'm grabbing ⁿes.

Sit back and ask yourself this, "Am I living my life to full potential?"

The lasting measure of a man is not what the world thinks of him but what his actions teach him. We create our own destinies, take our own measures, and cannot face hardships or seek the meaning of life without becoming whatever we expect to find. Therefore, any man even under crude circumstances can decide what shall become of him-mentally and spiritually.

There is an underlying reason for everything.

I know I'll have more bad times in my life, but next time someone say's "DON'T FORGET EVERYTHING HAPPENS FOR A REASON", I'll know it's true. We all go through bad times in life; the important thing is to know that sooner or later that reason will come to you. When it does you will find yourself better off than you did before.

It can be difficult to define **wisdom**, but people generally recognize it when they encounter it.

Wisdom doesn't just come from experience alone; it comes from learning as well. If you don't learn from a situation, you are destined to repeat it. If you don't learn from anything, it wouldn't be called wisdom...now would it?

If a man or woman doesn't do right by their children, nothing in his or her life will truly blossom.

Children respect those who took the time to love and nurture them. Do right by your kids. Get involved in their education, in their daily life. Dig into their daily lives even if it means setting aside some of your other obligations. There is really nothing more important or more rewarding than raising a child and watching them grow into a healthy, productive, self-reliant individual who confidently, but humbly walks in the world. No part of life would allow me to bring children into this world and not be responsible enough to do my duty as a parent. If I were to be selfish and lead my life as though I didn't have children I don't believe GOD would bless me to have a beautiful life.

Appreciate everything; take nothing for granted.

Some people are never satisfied by what they get or the help they receive. They always think they can do better or get better things then they already have. Learn to appreciate what you have, your life will be better.

Always remember, "Storms don't last forever so hold on, you will rise."

There is a potential for adversity in anything we do. You can be caught in a downpour at any given moment. The key is to brace for the storm.

Do not allow others to cloud your judgment or crush your dreams.

Happy people basically focus on others. Unhappy people focus on themselves and wallow in self-pity and doubt. Grateful people are far more optimistic and see whatever circumstances they're in as an opportunity for good.

Think creatively... Think passionately...Think strategically...Think quietly but most of all Think!

It's important to always focus, remain calm, analyze the situation, and think carefully before making any decision that would impact your life. Think before you act on something, as you may not get a second chance at correcting it.

Trust your instinct; it will never lie to you.

If you feel right about something and you second guess it, chances are you were better off with your first instinct. I always find that my first gut instinct is the right one. Trusting our natural instinct is our key to survival.

You can learn a lot by just observing.

Observe everything! People can show you better than they can tell you. Improve your skills of observation, never underestimate or overestimate any one or any situation. Therefore learn to read people by just watching them.

Don't confuse arrogance with class.

Arrogance is a matter of self-esteem, and is often offensive, loud, boisterous and inaccurate. There is nothing wrong in knowing your strengths. There is however an offense in implying your greatness and wielding grand illusions of power as a cover for a sense of fear and inadequacy. False pride looks foolish, but to know your own strengths while always remaining calm and collective is confidence and in my world classy.

Never lower your expectations for anything
or anyone.

If you expect to have something, be something or live by a set of rules and principles you deem right for your life, let nothing or no one make you change. If you lower your standards and expectations you will regret it and wind up living with resentment until you set the bar high or higher than it once stood before.

Little knowledge is very dangerous.

If you have no knowledge of self, no history of whom or where you come from, you are endangered.

To be idle requires a strong sense of personal identity.

Patience is the ability to idle your mind, to block out all the noise and worldly attachments. When I'm idle, I'm meditating or in deep thought for my greater good.

If you're the only one shining in your camp, that's not a team, you are a self server with a bunch of yes men.

What merit should an entourage have to grown men? NONE! Especially of those who hold no purpose or meaningful use other than agreeing with everything the bread winner says. Pull up your pants, find dignity and self respect. Stop selling yourself for nothing other than to fit on a team you hold no stake in.

Ultimately it's not about winning, but it is about reaching within the depths of my capabilities. My path to greatness is responsibility.

When you have much to accomplish you must direct your course and be responsible for your actions. We are responsible for what happens to us and the positions we put ourselves in.

To be a star, you must shine in your own light, follow your own path, and don't worry about the darkness. For that's when the stars shine brightest. I had to learn every path has its puddle.

We all hit a wall or trip over stumbling blocks along our way. Get up! Break that wall! Let nothing stop you if you know within your heart and soul you are meant to be something more than average. Make it happen! Now!

Some people are truly lost when they think status, power, or money will save their soul.

No one on this planet will be judged differently on judgment day. Your rank, privilege, or status matters not. If you believe you will be, you're just as foolish as the bubble you live in.

You can't buy peace of mind.

Peace of mind...you can't buy. Even if you had all the gold from King Solomon's temple, that won't bring you peace. A lot of rich people don't have peace of mind. Trust and believe. Peace is priceless. Now breathe slowly and deeply. Clear your mind and never lose sight on what's important.

Never lower your expectations for anything or anyone.

You're not in this world to live up to anyone's expectations but your own. You set standards for yourself and you live by those very self given moral laws if people expect you to break your moral laws, remove them from your life immediately.

Lead or get out the passing lane.

If you can't lead, you will have no choice but to
follow. What else is there really to say about this?
People who are honest with themselves go far in life.
People, who are not, stay behind the leader. Don't just
follow or wish to lead...lead!

When you roll the dice, please know how to play the game.

Learn the rules of the game and play it like a champion. Whatever game or sport you chose, become the very best.

Man's greatness lies in his power of thought. Nothing great in the world has ever been accomplished without passion

Anything you want to accomplish, you must put thought, passion, and energy into it. Nothing great will come quick and easy. Many of times I had to scrap a project and start over. It was my passion that carried me to completion.

We tend to forget that happiness doesn't come as a result of getting something we don't have, but rather of recognizing and appreciating what we do have.

This world is filled with so much greed and temptation. It's easy for one to lose sight on the things that matter most. I had to learn to appreciate what I did have and what is essential to me. For some foolish reason we think the more we have the better off we are. That's so far from the truth.

Never sugar-coat anything. If a person can't handle the truth or constructive criticism, that's their problem.

Anybody who truly loves someone or cares about the person's well being will give sound advice. They may also say some things that the person doesn't like. Anyone sincerely there for you will not agree with everything you do.

What you find hilarious, I may find foolish. What you find exciting, I may find boring. What you find worthy, I may find it lacks substance. When you find yourself, then maybe we will see eye to eye.

You are who you are; I am who I am. You have the right to be different. You have the right to be who you want to be. If anyone has anything to say, tell them to, "get over it!" then read them this quote.

Don't fight meaningless battles with ignorant people, because in the end you wind up looking and feeling like the fool for giving them your energy.

There are people and some battles that just don't need your energy or effort. Because in the end of it all, you may wind up looking foolish or reduced to the level they wanted you to be all along.

The angry and the weak are to insecure to apologize.

People would rather remain angry to prove there point in a heated argument. Understand very clearly that you cannot beat these kinds of people. They are what I would call weak. Spitting angry words, reacting with extreme emotions, carrying about in foolish belligerent ways. Always remember, when someone is angry, it's difficult to reason with them. The bottom line is that if we decide to stay there in that anger, it will more than likely fester into something much bigger. People can't change people. Only God can change people. You may have a good reason to be angry, but don't use it as an excuse and don't take it out on people. When everyone calms down perhaps an apology will follow.

I'm very practical and my approaches to situations are very much thought out. I don't over or under analyze anything.

To become a master decision maker, or improve making decisions, you must think logically. Define what your goals are, then take the most logical plan to achieve them. While you will not always be right, you will be right a lot more than those who allow their emotions to do their decision making. Rather the outcome is favorable or unfavorable, it's for better to have made the decision logically & not impulsively or emotionally.

Know this, "Pride comes before the fall."

Pride and arrogance are destructive traits. Uncover your self-destructive habits before you destroy you.

The weak and inferior accept the status quo, but a leader challenges it.

I find that people are too often willing to except things because of circumstances. You don't have to be afraid to stand out. Be the one who will give change to those hopes.

The simple act of reflecting- pausing to consider or reason- can have a great impact on one's life.

I take my quiet time alone. I sit back and reflect on where I was and how far I've come. I think on my future and what actions I must take to get things done.

I crawled...then I walked...I crawled again ...and I walk once more. The hurdles will be there but this time I'm running to the finish line.

There were many ups and downs; highs and lows. There were times I didn't know what would become of me. But, I never lost faith or became hopeless. If you want to flourish, dial down the fear and the belief that others are so "in the know" or others can while you can't. You can and you will!

I am what I am. You are what you are. That doesn't make either one of us better than the other. The difference between you and I - "I'm not the actor."

Many of us know people who act as though they are someone other than themselves. It is harder to constantly have to put on a mask everyday to than show true identity.

A Snake can and will only hide in the grass but so long.

A snake to me is a non GOD fearing person, someone who doesn't consider or fear repercussions or consequences of their actions. One who has only one thing in mind, "satisfying self!" We all know or have known, or have come across someone like this. Eventually they will wiggle out into the open.

Unfortunately, some cannot honor a friend's success without envy. If you don't believe this, check the faces of those around you

Sometimes people unknowingly show their genuine feelings when looking on at the success of others around them. Some are genuinely happy to see a friend or family member shine. Then there are those who are not & their face expression says it all. These genuine displays of emotion are candid and cannot be changed unless you remove yourself from the envious. You see envy carries with it resentment toward the person who has what you don't. This, in turn, can lead to bitterness, hatred, and deceit, the joy of other people's misfortune. That's why envy is one of the seven deadly sins, not jealousy.

He said...she said...you said...they said. Well listen to what I say now, "Please mind your own matters and your own situations." You're positioning in life will be much greater.

People gossip for many reasons. It's usually due to insecurity. Gossip really bugs the hell out of me. However, sometimes even kind people can be found gossiping inadvertently in day to day chatter with friends and co workers. Rarely ever does gossip have any truth or validity. I really try to stay away from people who gossip, backbite or slander. Believe me, if they are freely talking about others to you, they will have no problem talking about you to others.

Never make false accusations.

Never accuse anyone if you don't know the facts, or you don't know the truth. If you don't know the difference, then you obviously need to have your head examined.

If you're destined to reign, then you surely will reign.

Work hard, stay dedicated, stay focused and you will reign. Oh yes, the question is, does anyone feel this way? Trust me, I have my breakdown moments but somehow in my mind something is telling me, "You are learning valuable life lessons. If you can handle this you can handle anything in the future. JUST KEEP GOING!"

Never tell anyone that you're great because what you're really showing is that you are weak…Greatness doesn't have to be told.

What is the true measure of greatness? Is it power or possessions? Is it money or wealth? Is it any of your accomplishments? No. It's what you do with what you have. How do you give back? How do you inspire others to be great? What will you do with your gift that GOD has graced you with? I know what I'm doing with mine.

If only I would've gotten there sooner.

Ever feel like you're always missing the boat? Ever feel you're a day late and a dollar short? Ever feel like it's too little, too late? After I undergo those series of emotions I am then left with the feeling, If only I should have, could have or would have. Oh to the lessons we learn.

I keep up with nothing but current events.

There is really no way to keep up with it all. If you keep trying to keep up with everyone else, you are going to be disappointed. We all want nice things but we should get them because WE want them and can afford to buy it, not because the next person has and you feel left out. My advice to anyone who feels as such...Get your mind right.

I walk like Martin…I think like Malcolm…
and I write like Langston…That makes me
spirited, powerful and innovative.

Martin, Malcolm and Langston are three of the most
important men I ever learned about. They gave 100 %
to their beliefs and so do I. As do I. I stop for nothing.
I have a duty and responsibility to myself, my
children, and those before me who paved the way for
me to be able to share my talents with the world.

I've been called a lot of names…some good… some bad. However there's only one name that suits me now, "Grown Man!"

Brother's, when did you become a man? How did you know? Have you had a defining moment where you came through something hard and declared to self, "I'm a man now? I ask the deep questions because many of these "man-boys" never grow up.

Will you know of your window of opportunity? Will you be willing to take the risk? Most importantly will you make it count?

Know this…The mere fact that you are here on this Earth indicates that you are worthy whether you believe it or not. Each and every person is blessed with a unique talent, a passionate purpose, and the wisdom to express their full potential.

Fighting against your heart can be very hard.

If you are disconnected with who you are, at your deepest core is where you will struggle. If you are out of alignment with your truth and what your heart calls forth, you will find dissatisfaction, frustration, and desperation, I know because I've been there many times over. Keep looking, you're in there somewhere.

Never consume too much of anything.

If you're doing too much in one area, chances are you're not doing enough in another. Everything has a balance and when you throw the balance off, things aren't as good as they are when they are leveled. Obviously.

Think before you open your mouth or you might regret something you say.

One of the most obvious and significant attributes of man is the ability to communicate through speech. But for some reason we get people who don't think before they open their mouth. The goal is to be aware of when to talk, and what to say before we speak. Most importantly, knowing when not to speak at all.

If I did not offer to tell it, don't ask.

When people aren't actually addressing you chances are they may not want your opinion or your suggestions. Some people have a bad habit of over stepping in people's business. Don't be one of those people.

Logical and critical thinking is fast becoming legend.

Any decision you make in life should be based on "logic" not "emotion." Decisions made based on logic are decisions that are more likely to be right than wrong. They tend to be right because they are based on all available data and not your "perception" of this data. Critical thinking is nearly a thing of the past. People rather speak from an emotional state than that of a logical and critical thinker. As a result logical and critical thinking is becoming a thing of the past.

We can all make a difference.

People always have in mind that elected officials will get in office and make all the difference in the world. I think not! To make a difference is a collective effort by all! You're most basic constitutional right, is the freedom to speak your mind. You, yes you, can also help those less fortunate and this is what my freedom of speech is all about. Whether you are regularly involved in community, social, political and environmental causes or are new to attempting to change the world, it's possible...you can do it. Keep on trying. You can be sure that it's someone out there that will appreciate the difference you can make for them. As I said, "keep on trying!" Experience the true power of making a difference.

If some around you are constantly making poor choices and decisions you may want to opt-out the constant chaos.

The answers to this statement usually become obvious as time passes. No one has time to sit there and baby a person and their screw ups. Obviously they like to screw up if they keep repeating the same things over and over again. These types of people will bring you more problems and drama than you bargained for. You can pray for them but other than that I suggest you stay away until they figure themselves out.

There is an underlying reason for everything.

I believe everything is predestined. Nothing occurs by chance. Everything happens for a reason, good or bad. If at any time one has experienced something that defies coincidence (and this situation is incredibly common), then it goes without question that the remainder of life is equally governed by such a law. That we forget life's little miracles of precise timing in the routine of everyday monotony keeps most people from paying attention to such principles as predestination. It takes a different type of person to accept that there is a higher intelligence guiding destiny.

Not every buddy has your best interest at heart. Not every so-called friend or family member wants you to succeed.

Not everyone is a good friend or family member; nor do they all want the best for you. Sad to say; but true. Some people have the ugliest relationships that their potential goes with their accuracy-UGLY! Believe it or not, some of your friends and family members are hoping that you fail because your success is their failure. It reminds them of their laziness and their poor work ethic. Sometimes it's best to just fly under the radar and keep your goals and achievements to yourself. It would be more pleasant if you didn't have to do this, but unfortunately we live in a world of hate and it consumes many.

A relationship with no trust is just like car with no oil...Stalled and going nowhere.

No relationship can ever last if there is no trust...may it be personal or business..."PERIOD!"

Don't worry about others; mind your own business and worry about yourself. It's one of those lessons we all seem to forget as we get older.

It can be very irritating and frustrating when others feel they just have to butt in to your life. It's really frustrating when others want to constantly know what you're doing where you're going, and why you're doing whatever. Unreal! Mind your own business! It can't be that hard.

Don't let fear consume you...Remain strong and faithful.

When fear grips you and you allow it to dominate your life, you began to live on tippy toes, trying hard to step into the safest forms of life we can bare. Some might say fear is good because it stops us from doing stupid things. I have come to believe that it actually stops us from doing great things. Step out on faith. Learn to be afraid of the unknown. Listen, everyone fears something; you're not the only one who has fears.

Don't allow others to cloud your judgment or crush your dreams.

Happy people basically focus on others. Unhappy people focus on themselves and wallow in self-pity and doubt. Grateful people are far more optimistic and see whatever circumstances they're in as an opportunity.

Adversity is a great teacher. Did you learn the lesson?

I've been to hell and back…Life is real! You've got to keep your faith and believe my people. It's never too late to make it back.

You're calling, talents and abilities lie on one
path. It is your job to find that path.

That one thing you like to do could be something big.
The passion that you keep tucked away. That one
thing that you keep discounting about yourself can
have limitless possibilities if you were to embrace it
and go forward. Writer, fashion designer,
motivational speaker, actor, anything you know you
were put here to do, do it. Pray and push forward.
Take your talents and abilities and grow. Trust me,
there's nothing like the feeling you get when
investing in yourself.

Building self esteem and self confidence is the key to happiness and success. With belief in yourself nothing can stop you.

Self-esteem is all about how we feel about ourselves. We may not feel valued, loved, accepted, and thought well of by others, but try not to let yourself be ruled by the opinions of others. I don't care who it is. People with healthy self-esteem are able to feel good about themselves, appreciate their own worth, and take pride in their abilities, skills, and accomplishments. People with low self-esteem may feel as if no one will like them, accept them or anything they accomplish…Most of the time these people will make fools of themselves trying to prove who they are to others. We have to value, love, and accept ourselves.

Money does not make you great. You would have to be great already. Otherwise you will be just a hollow piggy bank.

Money doesn't make you good or bad. Sure you can buy nice things...nice perishable items. Then what? Are you the type of person who would give back to those less fortunate? Will you build a community center in your childhood neighborhood? Will you become someone great or shallow with all the money and riches you've attained? What you're going to do is already in you...regardless if you have money or not. Again, money doesn't make you good or bad. However it will magnify who you are. Money is a tool, a vehicle in life. If you are greedy and become very rich you will not become less greedy but rather more greedy. Contrarily, if you are generous and become a millionaire you will not become greedy but rather you will have a greater platform to be generous. What substantive things will you do once you have the money is the question I would be asking myself. Money can be powerful only if you do the right things with it.

Learn to keep it real. If you can't do that, you will be taught to keep it moving.

I seriously can't stand fake people, talk constant trash about someone to anyone who would listen. Latter they try to become best friends with the very person you're back biting. UNREAL! I don't get involved with such malicious behavior. I find insincerity to be highly offensive. Nothing triggers me more than a fake and phony person, trust me they can't hide themselves for long and eventually would bite you…it's just a matter of time. Listen, "when someone I interacted with had a false and negative vibe about them. I actually took pride in the fact that I could see right through them" There was a time, I really felt like I was surrounded by people I just could not trust. An ugly scene, invisible knives in every one's back. It will be in your best interest to avoid the unauthentic insincerity of people.

To the men who strive to be gentlemen with morals…Listen; don't be bothered by the mocking words that come from foolish men. Always remember, "Boys understand so little."

The Peter Pan Syndrome mentalities stuck in lost eras, 30 - 60 year old boys who don't want to grow up has no use here. What can a grown man with morals possibly learn from these boys who obviously haven't grasped the essentials of life of being a man? Being a man involves taking responsibility for your choices, for your family, for your community, and for the generations of youth who look to you as an example. I don't want to live in extended adolescence as a 40 year old man and father of two. What kind of example would I be setting for my children if I did so? That I believe in fairytales and I'm an overgrown boy…PATHETIC! If you strive to be men you must take responsibility and grow up, NOW!

Act like a lady, think like a man. NO!!! Act like a lady, Think like a confident woman. Think for yourself because if you don't you will wind up destroying everything you were trying to build.

Women were not put here to think like men. If that was the case they would be one. Don't base your reality on that of a movie or that of what you see on reality shows. A man respects and loves a confident woman who's secure in her own skin PERIOD! The goal is for a man and a woman to complement each other --not compete against each other. The nature of a woman would eventually catch up her to her if she goes into something looking to act out the feelings she thinks that of a man would do. Listen, men are wired for competition. For the most part as soon as most men sense a challenge, it's all over. Women are not made to compete with a man; they just simply can't do it.

A leader must have the courage to act against a so called expert's advice. There's nothing more demoralizing than a leader who can't lead.

How can you lead the people when you can't lead yourself? Words are easy to speak. The double talk and actions of saying things to appease or ease...when you have no real intent, is not what a leader does. A good leader, instead of just saying what you must do, shows how to do it and stands up morally for what is right no matter the position it may seem to put them in. Weak leaders will constantly face trouble and issues. A good leader will have the respect and loyalty of their followers and will set an example model. This is the correct way. The leader isn't acting as if they are better than anyone else; they actually practice what they preach.

Blessings sometimes come in the form of lessons to be learned. If we really want the blessing, we must accept the lesson.

This may sound cliché but there is a lesson to learn in each and every situation. Many times we get caught up in the emotion of a situation not realizing we may be in this very situation for a reason which is to learn. We are to learn and we are to grow. I can assure you there's a blessing in the lessons even when we don't always see the reason, even if it's not to our liking. In time, we see it for what it is, a lesson learned. Only in time will we see it was for our greater good. Only in time we will have learned something and even grew a bit more.

If you're not willing to help...don't criticize or pass judgment.

First of all, if people have so many opinions about you and your actions such as what you should and shouldn't be doing and but are not willing to help you out on all these miraculous suggestions, tell them to, get the hell out of your face. Do you, like me, hate it when people criticize you? I mean, I can't tell you how many times I've been annoyed with know-it all people who criticize. When somebody judges, condemns, disapproves or, rejects you, withdrawals their approval of you. Say to yourself, "Who gives a damn!" Really! You don't live for the approval of others and you damn sure can't be judge by them at the end of your life. If anything I would stay clear of mouthy folk like that. Clearly they are not happy with themselves.

Life is not a waiting game. You can't turn it on and off and think opportunity will constantly be available at your convince.

Those who wait on big opportunities all their life rarely see success. Big opportunities often come from small reasonable goals. Think Big & be smart about it.

There are people that run their mouths a mile a minute. Be careful with those who constantly talk.

I was taught that if you don't have anything helpful or positive to say, don't say anything at all. The more you say, the more foolish you look. Always say less than necessary, especially when you're talking to me.

If you can't speak up for what you believe, you obviously are insecure with your ability to defend yourself or your beliefs.

Remove the shadow of doubt & speak up! Speak out and be heard. You may be the one who makes the difference. Don't let the fear of rejection crush your voice. For many people, the inability to stand up for oneself can be rooted from childhood. I would suggest some counseling and practice on learning to speak for yourself. There will be many times in your life where you will have to do so. It's inevitable.

Never judge a book by its cover. Read the book, study the book and you will probably learn something that can take you to new heights you never knew existed.

I don't like judging things I know nothing about. Doing that would make me foolish and ignorant. It changes things when you actually know the whole story. Right? It's always a good idea to observe, analyze then analyze some more before speaking /judging something you know nothing about or don't fully understand.

Difficulties strengthen the mind. Never let the armies of doubt hold you back.

Difficulties can make you stronger. If you set yourself on a purposely driven course to learn from the difficult times in your life, you will be stronger than you've ever been. The difficulties will draw you closer to yourself and more importantly closer to GOD. If you've never struggled or had to overcome something, how will you ever become self actualized?

Be motivated by the hate you receive and encouraged by the love you get.

Ironically haters don't really hate you. They hate themselves, because you're a reflection of what they wish to be. Let them be a fraction of your motivation. Stay encouraged by those who love you and pray; for your success.

My view on the word insanity and why some may need to receive this statement as nourishment.

Insanity is like continuously wasting your life and you have the power of a leader inside you. Insanity is like being stepped on, beat down, coasting through life miserably and you have this caged bull locked inside as well as the key to release it.

Change your inner story, and you change your outer life. Either way the power lies within you.

Do whatever makes you happy. Be sure to stay true to yourself and all of the prosperity and accolades will come naturally. Whatever brings you peace and happiness, at least one person will be there to enjoy it...you!

Yes everyday life can be a struggle. Overall life is too great to not appreciate. Move forward.

If you have a healthy high self-esteem you will allow yourself to achieve and enjoy what you want and know you deserve. If you experience a dramatic financial loss or traumatic experience, remember you will rebound. You will again create wealth and newer better experiences. It's as simple as that.

Take a look in the mirror. If you don't like what you see then start making changes. Face yourself!!! Remember other's see what you cannot!

Be accountable. Don't give up your power to change. I blame no one. I learned a man can be burdened. He can walk in mud or torrential rain. However nothing can stop his GOD given ability to shine. Adapt to change! INSPIRE!

Twisting the truth makes it a lie. If you have to twist the truth to make a relationship work in your favor, you are living a lie.

I really don't know why people do this. It will be better to tell the truth in the beginning. Don't hide anything from a person you claim to care about. Don't lead them on. Don't make decisions for them as to what they will and will not deal with. You can hide your true self but for only so long...the truth will always comes out eventually.

Do you know what it takes to get to the top? To gain recognition? I do… "Remain Authentic."

It's not easy being authentic. You have to be able to take some harsh criticism. That's because authenticity isn't popular. Instead fitting in is. But have you ever noticed the most successful, admired people are the ones who have vehemently gone against the grain? They have blazed their own trail and followed their own path? I know, because I am this! Authentic

There's a difference in being accepted for who you truly are and expecting people to tolerate your nonsense. Again, age doesn't define growth. Character does.

If you don't let go of what used to be, you'll never find out what's meant be. Don't live backwards; live forward.

Some of us experience some great times in life. It may be a pinnacle of happiness or keep sake of memories that we cherish forever. Sometimes when situations don't work out people tend to hold on and drag their memories with others into the lives of the person or situation they are in now. Staying chained to your past is not fair to the person you are with now. If you want to stay stuck and hung up on what used to be why drag someone else into it and chain them to your memories? Not fair. Listen, "nobody wants someone chained to another. If you stay stuck or keep going back, there is obviously something you haven't learned." Grab hold of yourself, break away the chains, and sever ties before you move on into a new life.

Let me tell you something, "If people seriously wanted to help you, it wouldn't be, "what's in it for me?" "They would help because they genuinely, sincerely care."

There's a right way to help someone and it's simply just to help them. No throwing their business in the street or expecting something in return. Just genuinely and sincerely help. Unfortunately most people won't lift a finger to help anyone unless they are getting something in return. I don't think that a "What's in it for me?" attitude sounds like a person who truly cares about your situation at hand. I don't respect shady people and I don't ask for help in the form of time, money or even a ride here or there, anything. I never expect anyone to help me with anything. They never have to begin with.

What should man hold indefinitely close to his moral being?

Moral values, Goodness, purity, truthfulness and humility.

Money, Power, Brains nor Intellect ensure greatness. If you believe that it does you may be out of touch or just plain stupid.

Let's say you have the dynamics in the quote above, it doesn't ensure that you will be anointed greatness. We live in a world of status and privilege where everything is measured by what you have or have not. Greatness cannot be bought or sold, but it can be learned. The path to personal greatness, whatever that means to you, is much more valuable If one strives for excellence and has the passion to push themselves towards greater good (nothing worldly) they usually will capture it with both hands. Greatness is not given, it's earned, usually you're your blood sweat and tears and pushing yourself most times to the outer limits of mind, body and soul while remaining humble, genuine, true to self and all those in the world. It may not be as easy as 1 2 3 but definitely not hard either. Every single one of us can achieve greatness. We need to set goals/ targets and have the passion and ability to push ourselves to greatness al while inspiring and motivating others.

When it comes to things you care about, leave nothing to chance.

"Leave nothing to chance!" Account for every possible outcome in your preparations for a better life. Ensure that everything goes according to plan. Make sure that everything goes exactly the way you want and expect it to. Don't sit back and wait to see what happens. Pray on you're preparations and then make the necessary moves to take control over everything you want and leave nothing to fate.

Check your celebrity at the door; it means nothing! "We all are equal in this house."

Honestly I could care less of how important people think they are or what level of status they may hold. Once you walk in the door of my house, we all are equal. You can be a homeless man, an academy award winner, judge, jezebel, lawyer or a United States Senator. It doesn't matter. We are all human beings and around me all will be treated equally.

Prayer, meditation, and belief I believe is the road to peace.

I flow with whatever is happening and let my mind be free. I meditate. I remain quiet and I stay centered by accepting whatever I am doing. I believe he who has mastered himself is truly in control.

I try to remain a man of few words, but if there is ever a time I should speak, the words will be powerful.

I'm a man of honor. I'm a man of respect. I'm a man of morals most can't match. I DO NOT discriminate RELIGION, RACE, WEIGHT, or PREFERENCE. Also a person is not measured on the material they have! You are judged by the contents of character in my eyes. BOOM!

Brothers! Thirty-five to Forty-five years of age, we are the brothers of generation LOST! All we know is deception, betrayal, back biting and self gain at the cost of whatever or whomever. The word loyalty is pretty much nonexistent. Although there are many good men here, it's rare to find one who's a gentleman as well. So when you meet one learn from him, appreciate him. I know who I am. I AM LEGEND! My brothers of the generation, who are you?

How can you know where you belong if you're scared to try?

There is no other way to figure out where you belong than to make time to do it and give yourself space to fail, give yourself time to be lost. If you think you have to get it right the first time, you won't have the space really to investigate. You might even convince yourself that something is right when it's not. As a result a quarter of your life is in crisis because you realize that you lied to yourself so you could feel stable instead of investigating the time and effort in correcting. Don't be scared. Instead keep on trying.

Being around those you can interact and learn from is the key.

If I can't grow or learn from you, why do I need to be around you? Have you ever wondered why you have difficulty learning from a particular group or circle of friends you associate with? The thing is you have learned something from them, "there's no room for growth here." If you want to grow beyond what you already know you have to make changes. It's nothing personal. All are not meant to walk with you as you grow.

If you don't have power to reason, power to understand and power of compassion, you're a loaded weapon waiting to explode.

My people, this isn't very hard to figure out. Look at all the crime, all the lawlessness, and all the lost people who just don't care about anything they do or the people they hurt. It's an Epidemic of monstrous proportions.

If you find yourself always jumping with the
same people, you may want to get away from
that exclusive behavior and become inclusive.
You will thank yourself for it, later.

Avoid unhealthy influences in your life, in order to
truly create the lifestyle you want. Some people may
have to go because of their negativity. It may be very
hard considering how close you may be to them but it
has to be done, you will be much better off. As sad as
it may be to see them go, it will be a major part of
your change. In fact, I strongly recommend getting rid
of any sources of negativity that seems to hover in
your life. It'll make you a much better person

You may try to drag me, beat me down and assassinate my character but I will rise in victory.

I wouldn't be able to destroy someone, even if I've been extremely angry. However, I'm wondering if people who try to destroy other people's character and situations should have it done back. When a person does you wrong is it immoral or wrong to want to get them back? NO! Trust me, they will get have their day. Besides, your success will be more sickening & burdensome for them to bear. Pray for the sick, twisted, demented, evil, doers.

If you don't know where you're going, how will you know if you've arrived? What are the signs of enlightenment according to you?

Selfish or Selfless; you're either one or the other.

I aspire to be selfless. I genuinely care and want to be a force of compassion. My impact has to be that of greater good. I'm grateful for everything I have and I do what I can to give back.

You are the source for your happiness.

We are all born with human emotions. It is in our makeup and our general disposition that dictates which emotion comes forth. Our emotions are also affected by the circumstances of our lives. Our makeup will determine how we deal with those emotions and the circumstances of our lives. That said, those emotions are indeed innate. You chose how to show them, when to show them and whether or not you will acknowledge them. Trust me!

It's never too late to explore possibilities. It's never too late to change one's life.

Remember this always, it's never too late to change your life. You can't change the past, but your future is waiting for you. If you're tired of the life you're living, change it.

You know there's an old saying which some need to live by. "Stab me in the front at least I'll see it coming."

Cowards! These are the people who go behind your back and betray your trust. All I can say is "be real!" If you want something I have or had a connection with, let me know. Don't stab me in the back. I find that to be one the most cowardly acts one could ever do. Betrayal and backstabbing is so common that you will be looked at as the one out of touch if you speak up about it.

Without spiritual strength, family support & friends who challenge you with love, one cannot help but give up, cave in or fall into isolation.

Everyone can feel lonely; including the most unlikely people you can think of can be lonely. So do not feel bad if you feel lonely. You are not the only one who feels alone in this world. If you think about it, everyone is alone in their own way. You're alone in how you feel, and who you are. But everyone is alone together? Do you see what I mean? Keep your faith; Keep smiling. Life's too short to live with sadness, regret or isolation. The world is very big, and it's easy to get caught up in things. Keep life happy while you still have it.

My knowledge, my experience, my well being and responsibility all come from one place-the ability to broaden my mind and intellect. I will never dummy down to converse with anyone you either walk away or meet on the level in which I speak. Understand the man before casting or judging what you cannot match

I know a little about a lot. This means I am an exceptional conversationalist and can communicate well with everyone. I believe that it's a stronger intellect that seeks to expose itself to opposite points of view. I am intellectually curious. Get with me!

Remember this always...all progress takes place outside the comfort zone.

I really dislike comfort zones. They keep you relaxed and off your toes. Most of us usually take advantage of being in a comfort zone. I like to always be on my toes, sharp and ready for whatever new challenges and/ progress awaits me. Comfort zones are the destroyers of progress and the lead cause of stagnation.

Now days, TRUST is like proving you didn't commit a crime. GUILTY! Until proven innocent.

One of the things I've learned is that people are either completely trustworthy, or completely untrustworthy. There are people in my life I know I can trust with certain types of information. Conversely, there are people in my life I absolutely cannot trust them with certain types of information. You have to learn who you can trust and what you can trust them with. All things aren't meant to be shared. Yes unfortunately people have to prove they mean no malice first. People can be rather dangerous with your information they know about you. You may have to treat all Guilty! Until proven innocent.

Some battles are not meant for you to win or lose...you are to learn from the lesson so the next time around you are well prepared.

We cannot win every battle, but that does not mean that we shouldn't fight hard or we should surrender. Yet, pick and choose your battles. Some are not meant to be won or lost but rather to learn the lesson.

Does your life experience mirror your internal self-esteem?

If you have an unhealthy low self-esteem you will never enjoy the life you dream of.

If you can't support me in the dark, how can you stand with me in the light?

If you can't support me when I'm down, there's no need for you to be there when I'm up on my feet. People will run out of your life faster than a speeding train when you're at the bottom of your struggles, but will return when they feel that you have something of worth that they can gain. Know the difference.

Conversation leads to inspiration depending on whom you are holding the conversation with.

We are adults! Ideally any, conversation we hold should lead to growth or help inspire you toward growing beyond what you already know. Otherwise there's not much to talk about.

I play no games in life. I take this very serious.

Life is life. My attitude, when facing a difficult situation, is "One day I'll die". Which sounds a bit over the top, but it really helps focus me on what I want. No second chances. Grab life and shake the hell out of it!

It takes maturity to understand that some situations in life won't go as planned; some things just aren't meant to be.

Things don't always go as planned in life. Delays will occur, disappointments will happen; people will get sick & die. Sometimes, we need to stop over analyzing the past, stop over planning the future, stop trying to figure out precisely how you are going to make things go as planned. Pray! Leave it with GOD. Trust in him to ensure you are on the path and course you prayed for. I've been there many times as I planned out my future. I had to learn and accept that things won't always go as planned.

While in the midst of building your world, take a single moment. Stop and let realization of how far you've come set in. It can change your world forever.

It's easy to get so wrapped up in the pace of our lives, in our endless to-do- lists, that we lose track of what is really important. It's not what we accomplish, how much we own or what we do. It's who we are, how much we love and how we touch the lives of others that truly makes a difference. Take a moment. Stop and smell the roses. Enjoy what you do have. By all means, continue to build your world. Most importantly take time to enjoy the world you have.

My thoughts become ink... my ink becomes inspiration...my inspiration will inspire this nation.

I love what I do! Inspiring people with my words is a gift from GOD I don't take for granted. I am thankful. If you have within you a talent that GOD has blessed you with, it's your duty to share, uplift, and inspire.

Hypocrites and falsifiers…there is a special place burning for you.

Do we really need to give a statement to this? Simply, "If you don't clean up your devilish ways you will perish."

You don't have to be unattractive to be an ugly person.

Being negative, mean, spiteful, obnoxious, conceited, selfish, shallow, lazy, abusive, dishonest, insecure, and concerned with only your outward appearance is pretty ugly. Learn to love yourself. There are more important things in life than having a vain screwed up personality that's prone more to hurting others is a very ugly person.

Nothing in life is worse than doing absolutely nothing.

If you want to accomplish anything in life you have get up and work hard. Dedicate yourself to your dreams, goals and aspirations. If you know you're meant to be something great you have to act on it. Don't sit there and do absolutely nothing. You will live with regret the rest of your life if you do.

Let no one put a period where Allah has put a comma in your life… Let no one write you off.

In this twisted world we live in people get kicks by stepping on others. It may be material, money, a tyrannical insecure boss/ supervisor, or a so-called friend who thinks they're better. Some people believe they actually have the power to write people off. Foolish ones this…"YOU DON'T!" You are mentally screwed up in your ways. Never step on people or make them feel less than. You will answer to this on judgment day. Think about all the wrong you've done to people. GOD can write you a one way ticket to a place you can't escape.

I will quietly dismantle any opposition.

Only a fool gives notice on what he plans to do. Informing the world of your every move is foolish, clownish, predictable, and downright stupid. Silence is always the best course of action you can take when making any moves.

Fear is a paralyzing emotion and if you succumb to it, it will have a negative effect on you.

I know I should conquer my fear rather than having fear to conquer my life. You have to realize that fear is an inevitable part of life. Once you can control your thoughts better and become the master of your own mind, fear then will be a very miniscule part of your life.

The more one judges, the less one loves.

People with negative attitudes are easily annoyed by people with positive attitudes. This may be because negative people are such easy targets. There's not much sport in taking them on.

World, I want to share something, a crush is to admire. Like is to desire. Love is to sacrifice. If you haven't sacrificed then I'm telling you right now, "You know nothing about love."

If you're one sided, selfish, self-centered and argumentative in a relationship you can't possibly know how to love let alone sacrifice. These words are very much foreign in your make up as a human being. You will be considered a nightmare to someone who has qualities to love and be loved in a relationship. And let's stop thinking my looks will carry me throughout the relationship; because truthfully they won't. Learn yourself before trying to give yourself to others.

Don't let an insecurity about something destroy your life.

Insecurity is a poor filter of information, resulting in false assumptions. Insecurity is the greatest enemy of healthy relationships. You must shift your core belief about the image you believe of self. Trust me I'm working on this as well. I have trust issues. I am careful of everyone that comes into my life. I had to look back deep to my core and locate the cause of my trust issues. I found them and I'm working on that part of my life. Good news! You can do the same.

Don't be weighed down by the contents of your baggage.

Our tolerance for stress is represented by the size of the things we deal with daily. Some of us have higher tolerance, because we have more things to deal with. The contents of our baggage can stem from the various stresses that we encounter every day. When the time comes and the contents of the baggage begin to overflow, things can turn sour. For example, we may feel fatigue, depression, ulcers, may want to turn to drugs or alcohol. The goal is to find ways to learn to cope. It's not easy, task but it can be done.

How can one speak on the issues and crisis that go on in someone else's life? Most of the time they're not even aware of what goes on in their own.

Those who seem to see wrong in everyone else's life, are too busy ignoring the wrong in theirs. I call these people bottom feeders. The people who feed off others misfortunes, hang ups, or struggles. Then they feed it all to other bottom feeders who would listen. Misery! They have many issues in their own life with an audacity to assassinate the character of others. I'm allergic to bottom feeders, so I stay clear of them anyway.

I don't believe in luck; I believe in reason.

I really don't like when someone says good luck. I'm not a mythical creature with a gold coin. For the most part, luck is coincidence. Those who believe in luck often look for signs of their good or bad fortune, and ignore evidence that might show them otherwise. Someone may wear a lucky football jersey that they believe is lucky because many good things happened when wearing it. While they're wearing it, they only take notice to the good things they encounter. Bad things happen, as well, but that seems to go unnoticed. If they take stock of the circumstances that brought about good and bad things in their life, they may figure out that old sports jersey had nothing to do with it.

The hypocrite takes good advice as an insult.
The feeble minded never learn.

I will never understand some people. They will ask
for your advice or what you think of a situation.
When you give them the answer and it's not what
they want to hear, they get mad at you. I'm thinking
they can't handle the truth. I'm thinking they are
glutton for punishment. I'm thinking they just plain
don't learn the lessons. How about you can sit there
and be foolish by yourself because nobody wants to
hear it.

The greatest natural resource you have is
YOU! Rise and Grind! Give this world all you
got.

You are the source of your happiness. You are the
source for anything that happens in your life. All
things start with your mental attitude. Faith and
inspiration is a must to achieve any goals. You have
these natural resources embedded within you.
Personal growth gives you the concrete steps you can
take to align your life with the core of your being. I
know personally that in the midst of suffering, all we
desire is relief. We are the only ones who grant that
relief we seek. Pray, focus, and work towards your
goals. Remember struggle does not remain forever.
Keep your mindset and attitude positive and you will
see the change you seek in no time.

Building self esteem and self confidence is the key to happiness and success. Believe in yourself. Nothing can stop you.

Self-destructive behavior doesn't have to be done on a big scale to be damaging.

I don't do things to get recognized as most need to do. My message is empowerment and I'm confident enough to believe in my ability to stand alone.

People do the craziest things to gain recognition and stature. Some hurt many people in their path because of their lust for the spot light. I learned long ago that you shouldn't hurt people for selfish reasons. Sometimes the intangible is the most permanent. How we make people feel is what matters, not showing off material luxuries. People will forget about your new car, your expensive Breitling watch, your fancy clothes and your big house; but they won't forget how you made them feel. This is my message of empowerment. Take heed because this is how relationships are built. Take heed because that is how we all find happiness.

Some people's self-worth revolves around that little burst they get from impressing others.

Don't spend your life trying to impress others. While we're here, we have to enjoy yet be fully responsible and accountable. Life will be so much easier if we would just stop trying to impress. Live for yourself and not others who most likely don't give a damn about you in the first place.

Be careful what you are actually expecting from yourself and of how you evaluate.

Expect greatness. Gain greatness. Your results will be great, when you expect them to be so. You also need to understand that you get back what you put out. So if you put nothing out, don't expect anything in return. You have to be real with yourself and with others. Nothing great comes to dishonorable people.

Don't settle for less than your worth.

Simply put, people will only treat you as well as you treat yourself. If you allow them to walk all over you and your feelings, it will be hard to get the respect you deserve. This is a zero tolerance statement. Don't settle for anything. Know your worth.

Instead of spending time promoting has-beens and what use to be in past relationships, take the time to invest and promote in now.

If the person you're currently dating or trying to know reminds you of their past relationships and what they once shared with others, you may be forced to leave them right where they stand. Stuck! Frozen in time! Next time they bring up the past you should tell he/ she to go back out with the Ex has- been. That's a big No-No in relationships. I would move on, and find someone that actually cares about me and not his/her ex. Would've, could've and should've are comments used when someone has a stuck mentality.

The good thing about knowing and being who you are is you don't always have to defend yourself or your position to anyone.

Knowing who you are makes you spiritually strong, and steadfast in life. To be happy you need to be satisfied with yourself. You need to know how to meet your needs. Being yourself living a life in a confident affirming manner. It is recognition that all people are different. No one way to 'be' is any better than any other, regardless of what others may tell and show you. Brush the fools off! You know who you are.

The disease to please is a poor approval habit; it's a hindrance to you and you're growth as a whole.

The definition of people pleasing is within the phrase itself – pleasing people. It is an attempt to please people, to satisfy people, to make people happy and comfortable by providing preferences, comfort, ease and assurance, just to name a few. There is no way you can please everyone so stop trying. You won't please everyone. You won't please one person all of the time. Hell. You won't even please yourself all of the time.

Don't make a decision for someone as to what they should or should not accept. You can, however, explain your situation. Give them the truth fully & let them make their own mind as to what they will and will not deal with.

People have a bad habit of leaving out crucial information or omitting certain details that you need to know while you maintain any level of involvement with them. All I can say is, "watch out for these types of people." Make sure when you learn of their secrets or hidden situations remove them from your life.

When the darkest of days and trials are upon you and at their greatest, do you elevate yourself to another level? How do you handle adversity?

Author's Note

This book of inspirational and motivational quotes and sayings are of everyday life. Use this book as a tool or guide when you second guess yourself or think you're alone in what you go through. "Trust me, you are not alone."

Acknowledgements

Thank you to all who have read this book. May it be helpful to you as it is to me during difficult times and various stages in life. May it be inspiring, encouraging and uplifting. I also would like to acknowledge all who inspired many of the quotes and sayings. Good or bad, it has taught me much. I thank you. Sincere gratitude to Editor: TMT. Cover Designer: Baja Ukweli. Logo Creator: Serron Green. Thank you all for being insightful, smart and a great team to work with.

Esham Abdul Giles

Quote Me

21113465R00109

Made in the USA
Charleston, SC
06 August 2013